How Children Learn
a Second Language

by
Kenneth M. Johns

Library of Congress Catalog Card Number 88-61696
ISBN 0-87367-278-X
Copyright © 1988 by the Phi Delta Kappa Educational Foundation
Bloomington, Indiana

This fastback is sponsored by the Mid-State Oklahoma Chapter of Phi Delta Kappa, which made a generous contribution toward publication costs.

Table of Contents

Why We Need to Know About Second Language Acquisition

Within the past several years thousands of people from Latin America, Southeast Asia, and other non-English-speaking countries have been flocking to the United States for a variety of reasons. These people, together with non-English-speaking native Americans, have created a need to provide English-as a-second-language instruction (ESL). The challenge presented concerns not only the ESL specialist but also the regular classroom teacher. It is not uncommon nowadays for a child to show up on the school's doorstep some morning not knowing one word of English.

Teaching this child English presents a very real problem for the regular classroom teacher, who may or may not have the backup of an ESL specialist. Rather than approach the situation with a hopeless "What am I supposed to do with this kid?" attitude, it behooves the teacher to plan for this eventuality by finding out how children acquire a second language and by exploring the linguistic foundations on which sound ESL curricula can be developed. This is the purpose of this fastback, which is intended for the regular classroom teacher, not the ESL specialist.

Language Acquisition Versus Language Learning

In order to understand how children develop fluency in a second language, it is first necessary to differentiate between the terms "language acquisition" and "language learning." This distinction is important because acquiring a language is quite different from formally learning a language in the foreign language classroom. Language acquisition in children is a subconscious process in the sense that they are not aware they are acquiring a language and they cannot describe the rules for its usage. What they are aware of is a "feel" for the language and that language is used for communicating. Language learning, on the other hand, requires formal knowledge of explicit rules; and the learner is thought to profit from error correction. Error correction supposedly helps the learner master the correct representation of the rule. However, it is important to note that error correction does not help subconscious language acquisition.

Language Learning

Historically, the method for learning a second language in high school and college has been the *translation* method. This method, stemming from the study of Latin, is based on the notion that the scholarly way to master a language is to learn rules of grammar and verb conjugations. Although this method continues to be used, it is clearly inappropriate for young children who are neither scholarly nor very interested in learning rules of grammar.

In the 1960s, language teachers developed new methods for second language learning based on B.F. Skinner's behaviorist theory of learning. Called the *audio-lingual* or *aural-oral* method, it stressed the techniques of mimicry and memorization. Pronunciation exercises, pattern and substitution drills, and the use of language labs were activities typically associated with this method. This method also continues to be used but has fallen into disfavor for teaching young children a second language, because it requires the production of language in speaking and writing from the outset. Young children (or adults for that matter) are unable to respond in a language until they have experienced a substantial amount of listening. Forcing production in a second language causes many learners to become anxious, resulting in frustration and poor performance.

Because of the inadequacy of the translation and audio-lingual methods, language teachers have developed a new research-based method of language learning, called the *natural approach*, which has been found to be more appropriate for children. Using this approach, children are able to *acquire* a second language rather than learn a second language.

Language Acquisition: The Natural Approach

Whether acquiring a first or second language, there seems to be a universal order in which certain linguistic structures are learned. For example, the types of errors that Spanish, Chinese, Japanese, and Norwegian children make while learning English are strikingly similar despite differences in their first language syntax.

In addition, non-English speakers acquire English grammatical structures in a predictable order, and specific structures seem to be acquired earlier than others. For instance, certain regular inflective suffixes such as /ing/ verb endings (as in, Mortimer is eating worms) and the regular plural /s/ (as in, two fat hogs rolled in the mud) are among the earliest acquired. The singular possessive /s/ inflection (as in, Wally's hernia was giving him trouble) comes as much as a year later. This is not to say that the order of English syntax acquisition is the same for all learners. There is always some variation because of individual idiosyncracies or a person's first language orientation. However, there is enough similarity in the order of language syntax acquisition to establish an "average" order.

A further distinction between language acquisition and language learning is that language acquisition lays the foundation for fluency in the second language, whereas conscious language learning is used only to monitor for appropriateness of language usage. That is, conscious learning is used to make corrections or to change the output of the acquired system either before or after a person speaks. For example, if a person says, "I just eated the last cupcake," and realizes the error, he can correct the word "eated" on the basis of some previously learned rule. To be able to do this conscious monitoring or editing process requires three necessary conditions: First, the acquirer must know the rule. Sometime prior to making the error he must have become aware of the "correct" response and consciously incorporated it into his language schema. Second, he must be thinking about correctness (focusing on form) rather than on communicating. Third, he must have time to recall the rule and apply it in the conversational context. And all this must be done in an unfamiliar language!

Thus it is not enough for a second language speaker to realize he made (or is about to make) an error; he must also know the rule well enough to correct it. During ordinary conversation there is seldom enough time to consult consciously learned rules, so the monitoring process is of little value. Figure 1 summarizes the differences between the learning versus acquisition approaches.

Primary Language Acquisition

Before second language acquisition can be fully understood, it is necessary to know something about the sequence in which one's primary or first language is acquired. Most proponents of the natural approach to second language acquisition subscribe to the theory that

Figure 1. Differences between the learning vs. acquisition approaches

Learning

1. Focus is on the forms to be mastered.

2. Success is based on the demonstrated mastery of language forms.

3. Forms are learned for later functional applications.

4. Lessons are organized around grammatically based, contrasting analysis types of syllabi.

5. Error correction is a critical feature to promote the mastery of linguistic forms and structures.

6. Learning is a conscious process of memorizing rules, forms, and structures, usually as a result of deliberate teaching.

7. Rules and generalizations are taught deductively or inductively.

8. Lessons are characterized by teacher-developed drills and exercises.

9. Students develop the four language skills by following a teacher-directed calendar.

10. Early emphasis on production skills may produce unnecessary anxiety in students in initial stages.

Acquisition

1. Focus is on the need to communicate a message.

2. Success is based on getting things done with language.

3. Forms develop out of communicative needs being met in real-life contexts.

4. Lessons are organized around the needs, desires, and interests of the students.

5. Students' success in getting things done and in communicating ideas is the focus of reinforcement. Errors in forms are accepted as developmental.

6. Acquisition is an unconscious process of internalizing concepts and developing functional skills as a result of exposure and comprehensible input.

7. Rules and generalizations are not taught unless specifically requested by students.

8. Lessons are characterized by student-centered situational activities.

9. Students develop the four language skills by participating in functional communicative activities which allow the skills to emerge and develop naturally.

10. Lessons are characterized by low student anxiety as production and eventual mastery are allowed to occur on the student's own schedule after sufficient input.

Source: California State Department of Education − Office of Bilingual Bicultural Education.

children learn language by hypothesizing about rules and then test-
ing them in a social situation. They also agree that acquiring a language involves some sort of schema for passing from levels of lesser
to greater complexity.

The only purpose for children to learn a language is to communicate meaning. Because human beings need to convey meaning, they
grow up speaking language instead of imitating other familiar sounds
in their environment such as an electric mixer or a Mack truck. Clearly, the socio-linguistic environment influences the development of a
child's language functions. As children's social needs evolve, so also
do their language functions. Growth in language acquisition occurs
as the individual's varied functions in varied contexts call for increasing
flexibility and complexity of language use.

Halliday (1975) described seven language functions based on children's evolving social needs:

1. Instrumental: used to fulfill needs and desires (I want . . .)
2. Regulatory: used to control the behavior of others (Stop it.)
3. Interactional: used to relate to others, to establish and preserve
   ties with family and friends (Want to play?)
4. Personal: used to define self, express feelings, opinions, views
   of the world (I think that . . .)
5. Heuristic: used to find out about the world (Why? What's this?)
6. Imaginative: used to create, the language of make believe (Let's
   pretend.)
7. Representational: used to convey information (This is how it is.)

Some linguistic theorists speculate that language development occurs in a one-word, two-word, three-word progression. For example, even though a child may be able to conceptualize "Mama is
drinking hot coffee," his language will express only two elements of
the concept at the two-word stage: "Mama drink," "drink coffee," or
"Mama coffee." However, each of these three phrases has the same
meaning to the child.

Another view sees a child's language development as contingent on mastering the social context of thought. For example, at first the child uses words like daisy, flower, and plant interchangeably without making the semantic distinctions. But having taken a word into his speaking vocabulary, he learns by degrees to use it more precisely and for more purposes.

Still another position maintains that language growth is an abstracting and decentering process that involves increasing the distance between the speaker and the listener and between the speaker and subject. Here the language user moves from formulating private thoughts (reflection) to interacting with small, known groups (conversation), to communicating with relatively anonymous audiences (publication).

Jean Piaget's theory of language development agrees with the above but goes further. According to Piaget, young children go through two developmental stages in their use of language to think and to communicate. He calls these stages the *egocentric* and the *socialized*. Hennings (1983) has described these two stages of speech. Her examples of egocentric speech are:

1. Repetition: The child repeats sounds for the sheer pleasure of hearing them. These sounds may be words, but little meaning exists in the repetitive stream.
2. Monologue: The child talks aloud to himself without addressing a listener.
3. Dual or Collective Monologue: The child talks aloud in the presence of another person, but that person may not be attending and does not respond.

Examples of socialized speech are:

1. Adapted Information: The child can exchange thoughts with another person, saying things that might interest the listener.
2. Criticism: The child can comment on the activity of others, addressing remarks to others as part of general interaction.

3. Commands, Requests, and Threats: The child can tell or ask
   others to do things, addressing these remarks to others as part
   of general interaction.
4. Questions: The child asks questions, expecting answers.
5. Answers: The child answers questions and responds to the requests of others. This requires having listened to what was said
   and thinking about an appropriate answer (Hennings 1983,
   p. 39).

Although the various theories discussed above describe language
functions from slightly different views, they all see language development as the growing ability to fit one's language to a variety of audiences, in varying situations, and for various reasons. And they all
support the contention that children learn language by using it in natural, purposeful, and active ways.

By the time children reach school age, they have already developed quite a variety of language skills, and they demonstrate an ex-
cellent grasp of phonology, syntax, and semantics. Phonology is a
system of speech sounds within a particular language. Syntax refers
to the arrangement of words as elements in a sentence (word order).
Semantics deals with the meaning of words. School-aged youngsters
also are beginning to use language to control aspects of their social
system. That is, they become more and more aware of the function
of language and are able to use it to their benefit when interacting
with others. This social use of language expands greatly as the child
continues through the grades.

This brief discussion of how first language acquisition occurs serves
as a preface to the next chapter, which discusses how second language acquisition occurs.

Second Language Acquisition

Some young children acquire a second language in the neighborhood prior to starting school, but they are the exception. Most non-English-speaking immigrant families tend to cluster in a neighborhood of other immigrants, leaving little opportunity for their preschool children to encounter English-speaking models, except perhaps on television. On entering public school, these children immediately are immersed in a new and largely unfamiliar language environment, where acquiring a second language is necessary for coping in the classroom and on the playground.

By the time the non-English-speaking youngsters enter school, they already have a storehouse of concepts in their primary language. To some extent this simplifies the second language acquisition process. For example, the Spanish-speaking child comes to school with the concept of what is meant by "casa." His only task then is to "discover" the English equivalent — "house."

This idea has been formalized in a schema called the "dual-iceberg theory" illustrated in Figure 2 on page 16. In the schema, the "pool" of language concepts learned in the first language are shown above the surface of the water. The tips of the dual iceberg represent those obviously different surface manifestations of each language. They represent those elements of both English and the second language that must be acquired independently as completely new information. Below the surface are the common or shared language proficiencies.

Figure 2. The "Dual-Iceberg" schema for second language acquirers.

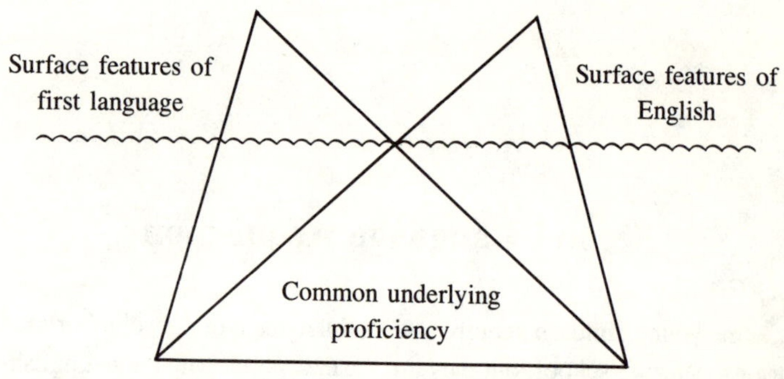

The reason these shared lingual proficiencies are shown below the "water line" is that the average person fails to recognize that many features in one language occur in another. For instance, it has been estimated that 80% of the reading skills taught in English also occur in Spanish. Structures common to both Spanish and English that many teachers do not notice include: sentences tracking from left to right and from top to bottom, letter/sound correspondence, and order of syntactical elements. In addition, each language has several cognates, or words from the same roots (for example, chocolate). Similarities between Spanish and English are illustrated in the following sentences:

English: I   go   to the store to buy   chocolate.
Spanish: Yo voy a la tienda para comprar chocolate.

Similarities also exist between English and other languages, especially Germanic and Romance languages. Commonality of language elements supports the proposition that second language acquisition may be easier than first language acquisition.

In pursuing his quest for second language fluency, the acquirer goes through four stages of development: 1) Pre-production, 2) Early Production, 3) Speech Emergence, and 4) Intermediate Fluency. Each of these stages will be discussed below with examples.

Pre-Production: The "Silent Period"

In this first stage or "silent period" of second language acquisition, the acquirer is concerned with receiving speech rather than speech production. Production of speech in a new language requires substantially more cognitive effort than reception because the acquirer usually must translate the message into his primary language before responding. The following illustrates the cognitive process required for speech production:

> *English speaker:* Do you know where I can find a shoe store?
> *Acquirer:*
> (Thinks) Hay una zapatería hacia abajo la calle dos cuadras a la izquierda.
> (Mentally translates) There is a shoe store down the street two blocks on the left.
> (Responds) There is a shoe store down the street two blocks on the left.

For most beginning acquirers, the "translation" process becomes overwhelming because they become preoccupied with form to the neglect of communication. But with the "silent period" stage there is time for the acquirer to concentrate on comprehending messages in the new language. Word and sentence formation are ignored for the time being because they interfere with comprehension. This is a time for getting acquainted with a new system of speech sounds, rhythm, and intonation. And it is a time for associating a new vocabulary with familiar concepts in one's first language. It is also the place where non-verbal language components like body language and gestures are absorbed.

Since the focus at this stage is on comprehension, the acquirer's responses are usually non-verbal ones like pointing, touching, and head nodding. Exposure to natural communication in the second language is necessary for the subconscious language processes to work. The richer and more frequent the exposure, the faster the acquisition process takes place.

However, mere exposure is not enough. The acquirer needs to comprehend the message in a social and meaningful context. Comprehending must come before speaking. Krashen (1981) calls this phenomenon "comprehensible input," which means that the learner acquires an understanding of the message but does not focus on or analyze the form of the input. Understanding does not mean being able to recognize every word or to interpret every syntactical structure, but rather to understand the essence of what is being communicated. Language containing structures that are not "known" can be understood by utilizing context, extra-linguistic information, and one's own knowledge of the world.

For speech to be a "comprehensible input" it must contain a real message and there must be a need for the message to be communicated. Speech that does not contain a real message and is presented only for the practice of some rule may be useful for some learning purposes, but it will not contribute to language acquisition.

One technique widely used in ESL classrooms is called Total Physical Response (TPR). With this technique, the instructor gives and executes a command such as, "Touch your nose"; and the class responds as a group by executing the command. Later, the same kinds of commands can be given to individual students. With TPR, no verbal response from the student is expected; only execution of the command is required.

Speech presented during this pre-production or "silent period" typically is language used in routine classroom management functions: "Stand up," "Take out your book," "Line up at the door." Other language used includes names of people close to the child, names of body parts, common classroom objects, and articles of clothing. Introductory TPR activites also might include statements that cover size, color, number, and location: "Put three, big, yellow pencils on the desk."

Pictures can be used in much the same way as classroom objects. The instructor describes what is in a picture and asks the group to identify certain objects. Pictures allow the teacher to expand language input beyond the immediate classroom; for example, a store or a zoo. Language input, using a picture of a farm scene, might sound like this:

Here's a new picture. What do we see in the picture? [without waiting for a response] A cow, a chicken, and a pig. Here's the cow [pointing]. Here's the chicken. And here's the pig [pointing again].

Who wants to hold the picture of the cow, the chicken, and the pig? [hands up] Gilda. Gilda is holding the picture of the cow, the chicken, and the pig. Gilda, point to the cow. [If Gilda does not understand "cow," the teacher points at the cow and repeats, "cow."] Gilda, give the picture of the cow, the chicken, and the pig to Jose. [gives picture to Jose] Who has the picture of the cow, the chicken, and the pig? [Jose] Jose, point to the pig. Show Gilda the picture of the pig.

In this exercise the instructor's primary objective is identification of particular farm animals. A second objective, however, is to reinforce the concept of possession: "Give the picture to . . ."

TPR should be used until all the children can understand the important words that are used daily in the classroom. Most children quickly acquire enough vocabulary at the recognition level to follow the teacher's commands without having produced a single word in English! And they have acquired some sense of how simple sentences are sequenced without any formal grammar lessons.

This pre-production or "silent period" stage may last from a few hours to several months. Generally children need three to six months of "pre-speech" activity before they are ready to advance to the next stage of language acquisition, early production.

Early Production

Speech emerges slowly but naturally at different rates for different children. At the early production stage, children move beyond listening comprehension and begin to communicate using one or two words. This stage follows the theory of one-word, two-word, three-word development in primary language acquisition. Initially these words and phrases are usually those that the acquirers have heard frequently enough to feel confident in producing. The first speech produced usually consists of high-utility words such as "yes," "no," "desk," and "pencil" or routine expressions such as "How are you?" and "You're welcome."

There are several strategies a teacher can use to evoke one- or two-word responses. For example, the teacher may ask, "What is this?" Or she may begin a statement and indicate by voice intonation that the child should complete the statement: "Is this a book? No, it's not a book. It's a _____." Questions requiring a dichotomous answer such as yes-no, here-there, and either-or also are appropriate at this level. Here the children are given an opportunity to say some of the words they can recognize. The easiest way to ask these types of questions is to embed them in the context of the interaction. For example, the teacher has several stuffed animals: a rabbit, a bear, a mouse, a cat. etc. She chooses the bear and says, "Is this an animal?" [Yes.] "Is it a bear or a mouse?" [Bear.] The teacher then throws the bear to pupil farthest from her and asks, "Is the bear here or there?" [There.]

The Role of Pronunciation. At the early production stage it is not necessary that children pronounce all words precisely unless a mispronunciation interferes with meaning. This is especially true with acquirers over the age of seven. Human beings have the potential of reproducing the sounds of any language in the world. From infancy the sounds unique to any language become internalized in a child's cognitive system through repetition and reinforcement. But those sounds that do not occur in a child's primary language become harder to reproduce as the child grows older. After the age of seven, the vast majority of people are never able to reproduce certain sounds exactly as a native speaker would. The older person acquiring a new language substitutes sounds he "knows" to approximate those unique to the second language. That is why adults like Henry Kissinger and Ricardo Montalban, who are fluent in English, have heavy accents. Preoccupation with precise pronunciation detracts from the acquirer's primary objective of communicating meaning.

Phonetic reproduction problems can be best illustrated by looking at common mistakes acquirers make. For instance, it is not uncommon for Spanish-speaking acquirers to intermix the /sh/ sound (as in sheep) with the /ch/ sound (as in cheap). This acquirer might say, "The farmer has two cheap," when he means, "The farmer has two sheep," or "the candy was sheap," when he means, "The candy was cheap." Such intermixing of sounds can be ignored as long as what the acquirer is saying can be understood from context.

Sometimes, however, correction of pronunciation is necessary. For example, Asian acquirers often switch the /l/ and /r/ sounds. The acquirer may say, "I rike flied lice," when she means, "I like fried rice." Here, the mispronunciation may confuse the message and subject the acquirer to ridicule by her peers. In this situation, correction of pronunciation is appropriate. The "rike" and the "flied" may not cause any communication problems, but the teacher needs to point out the lexical difference between "rice" and "lice."

The transition from the pre-production stage to the early production stage should be gradual and spontaneous. The teacher should encourage and guide the student to produce language but should never force performance.

Speech Emergence

At the third stage, speech emergence, children begin to speak in simple sentences. At this stage, the emphasis shifts from language reception to language production in the form of simple sentence patterns and short dialogues. At this point it is helpful for the child to memorize specific high-utility patterns without necessarily knowing the exact meanings of each of the individual words. Dialogues can be between the child and the teacher or between two children. A dialogue might proceed as follows:

A. What is your name?
B. My name is ______. What's yours?
A. My name is ______. Where do you live?
B. I live ______. Where do you live?
A. I live ______. What are you going to do?
B. I am going to ______. What are you going to do?

In addition to simple oral speech patterns, rudimentary forms of reading and writing may be introduced at this stage. The *language experience* approach is most appropriate for introducing beginning reading and writing to second language acquirers. Briefly, this approach uses the child's own language as the basis for reading and writing. Here the acquirer either writes or dictates to the teacher what he wants to say about a particular topic. The teacher then edits the text and uses it for reading material. Figure 3 shows the writing-editing process used in the language experience approach.

The advantage of this approach is that the second language acquirer encounters only those words in his speaking vocabulary when he reads. Introducing reading vocabulary prior to oral mastery puts an unnecessary burden on the second language acquirer.

At the speech emergence stage, the teacher can begin to use "how" and "why" questions when interacting with the acquirers. These types of questions require the student to respond in whole sentences rather than one- or two-word responses. Following are examples of using "how" and "why" questions:

Teacher: Why is the boy wearing that hat? (mortar board)
Student: He is going to graduate.

Teacher: How did the honey get into the jar?
Student: Pooh Bear put it there.

Figure 3. Language experience approach: The writing-editing process.

Step 1: The child writes a story from his own experience and imagination. In the example below, Ryan writes a story about what he thinks might be found in the attic.

Whats behind attic door?
Scary spiters.   ugly webs
black widdios old suckeisa
with dirty closes in the
old rings and Julry. flying Gosts

By Ryan, Grade 1

Step 2: The teacher accepts what the child has written, but edits the spelling, mechanics, and grammar to conform to standard English.

What's behind the Attic Door?
Scary spiders, ugly webs,
black widows, old suitcases
with dirty clothes in them,
old rings and jewelry, and flying ghosts.

Step 3: The child uses his own story as the basis for the reading text.

Another way of introducing dialogue and high-utility language patterns is through the jazz-chant. Jazz-chants are based on everyday situations and consist of a dialogue delivered in a rhythmic song-like form. A typical jazz-chant goes something like this:

Shhh! Shhh! baby sleeping-ing! (quietly)
Shhh! Shhh! baby sleeping!
What do you say? What do you say? (acting deaf)
I say hush, hush, baby sleeping! (a little louder)
I say hush, hush, baby sleeping!
What do you say? What do you say?

I say, please be quiet, baby sleeping! (quite loudly)
I say, please be quiet, baby sleeping!

The teacher introduces the jazz-chant by acting it out in a way that all the children can understand the vocabulary. If she cannot do it with words, she does it with actions. After the whole group goes over the jazz-chant about 20 times, the teacher divides the class into groups; and the groups take turns doing the jazz-chant like a choral reading. When the group has mastered the vocabulary and sentence patterns in the jazz-chant, the teacher can assign individual students to act out the piece. Following is an example of a jazz-chant assigned to a boy and a girl:

Girl: I gave it away.
Boy: You what?
Girl: I gave it away.
Boy: What did you say?
Girl: I say, I gave it away!
Boy: Gave it away?
Girl: That's what I say. I say, I gave it away!
Boy: Why?
Girl: 'Cause I wanted to.
Boy: You wanted to?
Girl: Yeah, I wanted to.
Boy: Why didn't you sell it?
Girl: Sell it?
Boy: Yes! Sell it! Sell it! Why didn't you sell it?
Girl: I didn't want to.
Boy: Why didn't you give it to him?
Girl: I didn't want to.
Boy: Why didn't you give it to her?
Girl: I didn't want to.
Boy: Why didn't you give it to them?
Girl: I didn't want to! I didn't want to!

The above examples show how the acquirer continues to receive "comprehensible input" while at the same time engaging in an enjoyable activity. Children's intonation and pronunciation improve, their vocabulary expands, and they produce longer and longer sentences.

Intermediate Fluency

At the intermediate fluency stage, the student engages in spontaneous dialogue and composition. Here the emphasis is on vocabulary development in both languages and learning more sophisticated syntactical patterns. Also, colloquialisms and idiomatic expressions are introduced at this level. At this point the student begins to "think" in the second language instead of conceptualizing in the native language and then translating into the target language.

At this stage there are many activities that can be used to promote fluency in a second language. The important thing to remember is that the activities need to stress speech production rather than focus on grammatical form or correctness. Verbal games are a highly motivating way to acquire language in a relaxed atmosphere. In mastering the game, students acquire new vocabulary and use it as they interact with one another. Action-type games such as "Simon Says" or "Mother, May I?" are especialy effective in generating spontaneous speech production in English.

Another good language acquisition activity is to engage children in talking about themselves, their desires, preferences, abilities, or feelings. Following are examples of how a teacher can initiate conversations or discussions in which students talk about themselves:

Desires. Halloween is coming up. You need to think of what you want to be, what costume you want to wear. On Halloween, I want to be a ______.

Preferences: I will give you several choices and I want you to decide which you prefer. We are going to plan a class party and you need to decide what we are going to do and what we are going to eat. Which do you like the best? Dancing or games? What kind of dancing? Which games? Pizza or dessert? What kind of pizza? What kind of dessert?

Abilities: I will tell you how to do something. Some things I tell you will be true and some will be false. You need to decide if I really know how to do it. Whatever you decide, you must tell me why you decided what you did. [Teacher gives directions and ingredients for making a cake using, among other ingredients, pickle juice, chili powder, and super glue.]

Feelings: I will give you a "feeling" word. When I do this, I want you to think of where you are when you have this feeling. I am (teacher mimes "sick to my stomach") when I am _____. (Galyean 1977)

Other Factors in Second Language Acquisition

Krashen (1981) has pointed out the importance of affective factors in second language acquisition, especially anxiety, motivation, and self-confidence. Even if the "comprehensible input" is adequate, if the acquirer is under stress or emotional tension, little learning will occur. Acquirers of all ages need to be in a low-anxiety environment and feel secure if learning is to take place.

Motivation is another factor affecting language acquisition. Motivation may be *instrumental* or *integrative*. Instrumental motivation is what drives a person to acquire a second language for reasons of survival in day-to-day living. The acquirer is motivated to master English in order to communicate with people on the job and in the community — the merchant, the banker, the local bookie. Integrative motivation is less compelling. It is the desire to belong, to be identified as a member of the group. Most youngsters in ESL classes exhibit integrative motivation. They do not need to learn a new language for survival reasons, but they do have a strong drive to be accepted by their English-speaking peer group. Teachers should capitalize on this drive when working with ESL students.

As with most school-related tasks, the acquirer with high self-confidence tends to do better in second language acquisition. One aspect of self-confidence is a child's perception of how others view his first language. If the child feels that, in learning English, his native language is somehow inferior or not as good, it is bound to affect his self-esteem. Teachers must make a special effort to let children know that their native language is important and that they must continue to use it even as they learn English. Children should be told that knowing how to speak two languages makes them "special."

Dulay and Burt (1974*b*) have used the term *affective filter* to describe what occurs when acquirers are subjected to embarrassment, humiliation, and other negative responses when trying to learn a second language. In such environments the acquirer develops a "filter" that prevents him from internalizing the second language input.

Age is another factor affecting second language acquisition, especially at the intermediate fluency stage. Older acquirers generally make faster progress in the early stages of second language acquisition because of their instrumental motivation and their broader experience. In the long run, however, younger acquirers tend to attain a higher level of proficiency because of their lower "affective filter."

The Role of the Teacher
in Second Language Acquisition

The teacher of non-English-speaking children has three major tasks. The first is to provide a rich variety of "comprehensible input" related to routine classroom activity. The second is to provide sufficient practice of words or phrases used in situations outside the classroom so that the children can begin to acquire language from other sources. These sources might include peers, school staff, and other English-speaking adults with whom children have daily contact. Teachers should suggest to these secondary sources ways of modifying their speaking patterns when interacting with ESL students. The third is to create a low-anxiety atmosphere in which children can learn naturally without undue pressure.

As children move into the early speech production stage, there are several techniques the teacher can use to facilitate second language acquisition. Foremost is creating situations in which there is a necessity for the acquirer to communicate a message. By focusing on children's needs and interests, the teacher can structure dialogues or questions in ways that make the children want to respond with a personal message.

In communicating with ESL children, each message must be kept simple with only one idea in each sentence. The teacher must speak slowly and articulate carefully. However, this does not mean exaggerating to the point that normal speech rhythms and intonation are lost. Vocabulary should emphasize high-frequency words. When there are several words for the same thing, the instructor should choose the one in most common usage. Fused expressions like "hafta" (have to) and "shoulda" (should have) should be avoided, as should contractions (it's, can't, wouldn't, etc.). Use of appropriate body language and longer pauses at natural breaks helps to ensure that the message is understood.

The beginning acquirer has a tendency to look on English as an extension of his own language and thinks everything can be directly translated. For this reason, idioms, slang, and regional or ethnic dialect should be avoided. Such expressions as "He is off the wall" or "She lost her cookies" do not communicate what they mean if translated literally. Use of such expressions would be confusing to the second language acquirer.

Whenever possible, specific names rather than pronouns should be used. Instead of saying, "She gave it to him to give to you," the instructor should say, "Lupe gave the balloon to Elmo to give to Margarita." This use of specific names may seem awkward or redundant to a native speaker, but it communicates better to the beginning acquirer.

Clarifying the meaning of a word within the context of speech is another technique instructors can use. For instance, an instructor may say to a non-English-speaking child, "Have you been to the grocery store? You know, the place where your mother goes to buy fruit, vegetables, meat, and bread." Often key words can be repeated or rephrased: "Did you bring your lunch? Lunch, you know, what we eat at 12 o'clock, noon."

Also, sentences should be short. Avoid compound sentences and subordinate clauses. Instead of saying, "Give me the note that your mother signed giving you permission to go with us to the zoo," the teacher should say, "You know we are going to the zoo. Did you bring me (gesturing) the note? Did your mother sign (gesturing) the note?" By having the complex sentence broken into three short sentences, the acquirer is more likely to be able to comprehend the message.

Teachers should avoid, as much as possible, translating messages into the child's native language. If children have been exposed to extended periods of "comprehensible input," translation should not be necessary. This is not to say, however, that the teacher should not take an interest in the ESL child's native language and culture. There are many occasions in the normal classroom routine when the teacher can inquire about or make reference to the child's native language. For example, after a session when the children are learning the names of common classroom objects, the teachers might say: "You know that this is called a pencil. What do you call it at home? [child responds: "lápiz."] The teacher responds, "Oh, you call it a lápiz?" Another way of showing interest in an ESL child's native language is to invite the child to "teach" a few words or phrases to his English-speaking classmates.

Having a guest in the classroom who is a native speaker of the child's first language is still another way of fostering pride in the child's language and culture. Such guests might be a politician, a business person, or a local sports figure. The guests need not speak to the class in their native language. Just the fact that the guest is someone prominent in the community who is a native speaker of the ESL child's native language is sufficient to bolster the child's self-esteem.

In summary, the role of the teacher is to: 1) emphasize interpersonal communication, 2) accept all attempts at speech production without dwelling on correct form, 3) make no attempt to force speech production before acquirers are ready, and 4) take an interest in the acquirer's native language and culture.

Working with Parents and Other Caretakers

Caretaker refers to those responsible for child rearing in the home. They include parents, older siblings, relatives, extended family, and babysitters. Caretakers obviously have played a key role in the child's acquisition of his native language. Their role in the child's acquisition of a second language depends on their own fluency (if any) in the second language and on their attitude about having their children learn a second language.

Some non-native English-speaking parents, who recognize the economic and social benefits of knowing the dominant language in American culture, go to great efforts to speak only English to their children at home. This is unfortunate. By failing to use their native language at home, they virtually extinguish it in their children; and the opportunity for their children to become truly bilingual after a few years in school is lost.

There is ample evidence to show that the use of the primary language in the home is not a handicap to a child's acquiring a second language. On the contrary, research tells us that having a rich language experience in one's native tongue has a beneficial effect on second language acquisition. The point is, the more the acquirer uses language — any language — the quicker he learns English. So teachers should encourage the use of the native language in the home.

Schools should inform limited- or non-English-speaking caretakers of some of the things they can do to support their children's English acquisition process. Caretakers should be encouraged to tell stories, folk tales, sayings, riddles, and jokes in the child's native language. Also, caretakers can share with children records, photos, letters, and artisanry from their native culture. These objects stimulate immediate language use and concept formation, which facilitate "comprehensible input" when beginning to learn English. Caretakers can read stories from native language children's books and make these books and other printed material available for browsing. In addition, selective use of radio, TV programs, and movies in the child's native language can augment language development. These media can serve as springboards for discussions on issues affecting the family and can help develop critical thinking skills, which will be useful later when the child becomes more proficient in English.

Schools can encourage caretakers to have their children share aspects of their native culture such as foods, traditional celebrations, music, dance, and clothing. Opportunities to share their cultural heritage foster children's self-esteem and reduce their "affective filter."

Conclusion

Much research has been done in the last 20 years on how second language learning takes place. Among the central findings is that there is a certain order in which language structures are acquired. This "universal order" differs from the grammatical sequence traditionally used by foreign language teachers. Fluency develops gradually as a subconscious process. Formal learning of grammatical structure comes later.

In order for second language acquisition to occur, three conditions must be met. First, the acquirer must perceive a need to communicate in the new language. Second, the acquirer must receive "comprehensible input." Third, the "comprehensible input" must occur in a low-anxiety environment.

In acquiring a second language, children go through four stages: 1) pre-production, 2) early production, 3) speech emergence, and 4) intermediate fluency. Children move through these stages at their own pace. Forcing language production delays or retards progress.

The role of the teacher in second language acquisition is to structure an environment in which the acquirer finds it necessary to communicate. The teacher should use a variety of techniques so that the message transmitted is understood. Above all, the teacher should take an interest in the child's first language and culture and should accept all attempts made by children to communicate.

Caretakers should provide an environment rich in language experiences, where children can develop in their native language and grow intellectually. They also should cooperate with the school in its efforts to help their children acquire a second language.

When a non-English-speaking child crosses the threshhold into the classroom, it should be reassuring to the teacher that the child learned his first language without much difficulty and that learning the second is achieved in much the same way. All the teacher needs to know are some simple techniques suggested by research. And most importantly, the teacher can be effective without knowing one single word of the child's primary language.

References

Britton, James. *Language and Learning*. Coral Gables, Fla.: University of Miami Press, 1970.

Brown, R.; Cazden, Courtney; and Bellugi, U. "The Child's Grammar from I to III." In *Studies in Child Language Development*, edited by C. Ferguson and D. Slobin. New York: Holt, Rinehart, and Winston, 1973.

Chomsky, Carol. "Stages in Language Development and Reading Exposure." *Harvard Educational Review* 42 (February 1972): 1-32.

DeStefano, Johanna. *Language, the Learner, and the School*. New York: John Wiley and Sons, 1978.

Dulay, Heidi C., and Burt, Marina K. "A New Perspective on the Creative Construction Process in Child Second Language Acquisition." *Language Learning* 24 (December 1974): 253-77. (a)

Dulay, Heidi C., and Burt, Marina K. "Natural Sequence in Child Second Language Acquisition." *Language Learning* 24 (June 1974): 37-53. (b)

Dulay, Heidi C.; Burt, Marina K.; and Krashen, Stephen. *Language Two*. New York: Oxford University Press, 1982.

Galyean, Beverly. "A Confluent Design for Language Teaching." *TESOL Quarterly* 11 (June 1977): 143-56.

Gardner, Robert C., and Lambert, Wallace E. *Attitudes and Motivation in Second Language Learning*. Rowley, Mass.: Newbury House, 1972.

Gonzalez-Mena, Janet. "English as a Second Language for Preschool Children." *Young Children* 32 (November 1976).

Guskin, Judith T. "What the Child Brings and What the School Expects: First and Second Language Learning and Teaching in Bilingual-Bilcultural Education." Mimeographed paper provided by Lupe Romero, 1975.

Halliday, Michael A.K. *Learning How to Mean*. New York: Elsevier North-Holland, 1975.

Hatch, Evelyn M. "Discourse Analysis and Second Language Acquisition." In *Second Language Acquisition: A Book of Readings*, edited by E. Hatch. Rowley, Mass.: Newbury House, 1978.

Hennings, Dorothy. *Communication in Action: Teaching the Language Arts*. Boston: Houghton Mifflin, 1983.

Krashen, Stephen D. "Bilingual Education and Second Language Acquisition Theory." In *Schooling and Language Minority Students: A Theoretical Framework*. Los Angeles: California State University Evaluation, Dissemination, and Assessment Center, 1981.

Moffett, James. *Teaching the Universe of Discourse*. Boston: Houghton Mifflin, 1973.

Piaget, Jean. *The Language and Thought of the Child*. New York: World, 1965.

Slobin, Dan I. "Children and Language: They Learn the Same Way All Around the World." *Psychology Today* (July 1972): 71-74.

Smith, Frank. "The Language Arts and the Learner's Mind." *Language Arts* 56 (February 1979): 119-25.

Stevick, Earl. *Memory, Meaning, and Method*. Rowley, Mass.: Newbury House, 1976.

Stryker, Stephen. "Research and Second Language Acquisition." Speech made at the Eighth Annual Summer Bilingual Education Institute, University of Arizona, Tucson, June 1984.

Terrell, Tracy D. "The Natural Approach in Bilingual Education." In *Schooling and Language Minority Students: A Theoretical Framework*. Los Angeles: California State University Evaluation, Dissemination, and Assessment Center, 1981.